Dào dé Jīng
The Way of the Dao

Written By
老子 Lǎo Zǐ

Translated By
Thomas Hayes & 李思瑾 Li Sijin

First Published in Great Britain 2020 by Mirador Publishing

Copyright © 2020 by Thomas Hayes and Li Sijin

All rights reserved. No part of this publication may be reproduced or transmitted, in any form or by any means, without permission of the publishers or author excepting brief quotes used in reviews.

First edition: 2020

A copy of this work is available through the British Library.

ISBN: 978-1-913264-90-1

Mirador Publishing
10 Greenbrook Terrace
Taunton
Somerset
TA1 1UT

Acknowledgements

We are once again most grateful to Sarah and her team at Mirador Publishing. They have worked quickly and efficiently in the publishing of this book. They have been both flexible and courteous, acting with tenacity and good grace at all times. Unbounded respect and humble appreciation is accorded to Lǎo Zǐ and all teachers of the Dào, in whose steps we cautiously and in awe, tiptoe through.

About the Authors

Thomas Hayes

THOMAS HAYES HAS STUDIED and practised the Daoist Arts for more than thirty-five years. In addition to practising Chen style meditation, taijiquan and qigong, he also studies the Yì Jīng and other associated Chinese Daoist and Buddhist metaphysical systems. He has also cultivated under other Buddhist, Advaita Vedanta and Yoga traditions. He has qualifications in Stress Management, Life Coaching, Hypnotherapy and NLP. He is also a qualified TEFL teacher.

He works as a Data Protection and Cyber Security Consultant and is a Fellow of both the British Computer Society and the International Association of Privacy Professionals. He lives in Manchester, England. In addition, he runs an online company that promotes the very best of vegan products. He also provides help and advice in promoting Chinese and UK cultural exchanges.

This is his third collaborative book. His first, *Chen Tàijíquán: The Theory and Practice of a Daoist Internal Martial Art: Volume 1 – Basics and Short Form* was written with Master Wang Hai Jun.

His second, *Qi Baishi: An Introduction to His Life and Art: The Artist Who Is as Highly Regarded by the Chinese as Picasso Is in the West* was also written with Li Sijin and published by Mirador Publishing in 2017.

李 思 瑾　Li Sijin

李思瑾 Li Sijin has worked as an expert at the Qi Baishi Memorial Hall in her hometown of Xiangtan City, Hunan, for the last twelve years. She has undertaken the detailed translation of the subject with Thomas Hayes, her previous co-author of Qi Baishi. She has injected much needed effort and a commensurate enthusiasm into the production of this book. She lives and breathes the Daoist philosophy.

　　She is also a practicing accountant and an MC, hence she is a woman of wide-ranging skills and talent. She is especially interested in promoting the works of Qi Baishi and traditional Chinese culture in general to a Western audience.

Table of Contents

CHAPTER ONE	19
CHAPTER TWO	20
CHAPTER THREE	22
CHAPTER FOUR	24
CHAPTER FIVE	26
CHAPTER SIX	27
CHAPTER SEVEN	28
CHAPTER EIGHT	30
CHAPTER NINE	32
CHAPTER TEN	33
CHAPTER ELEVEN	35
CHAPTER TWELVE	36
CHAPTER THIRTEEN	38
CHAPTER FOURTEEN	40
CHAPTER FIFTEEN	42
CHAPTER SIXTEEN	44
CHAPTER SEVENTEEN	46
CHAPTER EIGHTEEN	47
CHAPTER NINETEEN	48
CHAPTER TWENTY	49
CHAPTER TWENTY-ONE	51
CHAPTER TWENTY-TWO	52
CHAPTER TWENTY-THREE	54
CHAPTER TWENTY-FOUR	56
CHAPTER TWENTY-FIVE	57

CHAPTER TWENTY-SIX	59
CHAPTER TWENTY-SEVEN	60
CHAPTER TWENTY-EIGHT	62
CHAPTER TWENTY-NINE	64
CHAPTER THIRTY	65
CHAPTER THIRTY-ONE	67
CHAPTER THIRTY-TWO	69
CHAPTER THIRTY-THREE	70
CHAPTER THIRTY-FOUR	71
CHAPTER THIRTY-FIVE	72
CHAPTER THIRTY-SIX	73
CHAPTER THIRTY-SEVEN	74
CHAPTER THIRTY-EIGHT	75
CHAPTER THIRTY-NINE	77
CHAPTER FORTY	79
CHAPTER FORTY-ONE	80
CHAPTER FORTY-TWO	82
CHAPTER FORTY-THREE	83
CHAPTER FORTY-FOUR	84
CHAPTER FORTY-FIVE	85
CHAPTER FORTY-SIX	86
CHAPTER FORTY-SEVEN	87
CHAPTER FORTY-EIGHT	88
CHAPTER FORTY-NINE	89
CHAPTER FIFTY	90
CHAPTER FIFTY-ONE	91
CHAPTER FIFTY-TWO	92
CHAPTER FIFTY-THREE	93
CHAPTER FIFTY-FOUR	94
CHAPTER FIFTY-FIVE	96
CHAPTER FIFTY-SIX	98
CHAPTER FIFTY-SEVEN	99
CHAPTER FIFTY-EIGHT	101
CHAPTER FIFTY-NINE	102
CHAPTER SIXTY	103
CHAPTER SIXTY-ONE	104
CHAPTER SIXTY-TWO	105
CHAPTER SIXTY-THREE	106

CHAPTER SIXTY-FOUR	108
CHAPTER SIXTY-FIVE	110
CHAPTER SIXTY-SIX	111
CHAPTER SIXTY-SEVEN	112
CHAPTER SIXTY-EIGHT	114
CHAPTER SIXTY-NINE	115
CHAPTER SEVENTY	116
CHAPTER SEVENTY-ONE	117
CHAPTER SEVENTY-TWO	118
CHAPTER SEVENTY-THREE	119
CHAPTER SEVENTY-FOUR	120
CHAPTER SEVENTY-FIVE	121
CHAPTER SEVENTY-SIX	122
CHAPTER SEVENTY-SEVEN	123
CHAPTER SEVENTY-EIGHT	125
CHAPTER SEVENTY-NINE	126
CHAPTER EIGHTY	127
CHAPTER-EIGHTY-ONE	128

Introduction

THIS BOOK IS WRITTEN during an extraordinary time for the world. It is the end of March 2020 at the time of writing the book. The Covid-19 Virus, also known as Corona Virus, is upon us. It is a major challenge to us all throughout the whole world. The virus is now close to its peak in the UK and hopefully, past its worst in China.

It is proof, is it not, that the world and the individual are inter-connected. Even Boris Johnson, the UK Prime Minister has contracted the virus. As I proof-read what I have written it has just been announced that others within the UK government have also been infected. We hope, by the time of publication, that they, and everyone else have come through these troubling times as unscathed as possible. We wish that they re-emerge in much better health, both physical and mental.

Our intention in writing this book is to present the 道德经 Dào dé Jīng classic written by 老子 Lǎo Zǐ to a modern audience. We have refrained from providing a commentary on each of the eighty-one chapters. Initially, this was our intention. We concluded, however, that to do so would be akin to putting legs on the snake as the Zen saying goes. This is because the words speak for themselves. As always, it is a balance between either saying too little, or expounding too much.

The Chapters that we have translated into English use the masculine pronoun 'he'. This was the convention at that time, and we have retained this. This approach is adopted merely to be pragmatic, circumscribed as we are by the restrictions of the written language. Lǎo Zǐ not only believed in the equality of the feminine and masculine genders, but actually wrote from a perspective that transcends this. We hope that nobody will take any offence at this concession.

The original version, attributed to Lǎo Zǐ, was written in the ancient Chinese language with its own associated characters. There also exists what is now known as Traditional Chinese characters. These are still used in the modern era in Taiwan, Singapore and Hong Kong. These characters are different to those that the ancient Chinese used, in terms of how they look and their number.

In. addition is what is known as Simplified Chinese. This is what is used nowadays in mainland China and is adopted for the Chinese component of this book. The written Chinese that we have used for to accompany the English translation is taken from a variety of ancient and contemporary sources.

Lǎo Zǐ is a title, rather than a name. It means 'Old Master'. He is said to have lived in China anywhere between the 6th and 4th

Centuries BC. There is also some conjecture as to whether he even existed at all. Some people believe that the classic work that we write about here is derived from a collection of individual Daoist Masters.

Actually, it doesn't really matter in the least if such an individual as is popularly described existed or not. The words and their significance are what we wish to reflect upon. Our intention is not therefore, to speculate on, or contemplate about the life of Lǎo Zǐ. There are countless such works already out there that already do so.

The Dào dé Jīng means 'The Way of Virtue". The Dào is not an object. It cannot be seen, because it is not made of form. Trying to find it is like the eyes trying to look for themselves. The best they can do is to be seen as through an intermediary, like the reflection in a mirror.

This Supreme State of Being or state of oneness with the Dào is something that is attainable by each and every one of us. It is not to be sought externally, although people inevitably attempt to do so. Neither is it something that should be regarded as holy or otherworldly.

It can actually, be experienced by everyone. It is already here, integral to our existence as human beings. If it was not, it couldn't be attained. Actually, it is not even attained, it is just to be realised. It is only unrealised because it is not observed by the ordinary consciousness, conditioned as it is to looking outwards at objects, rather than inwards to our very essence.

The mind must be totally free to merge with this so that there is no longer an observer and an observed but simply 'observing'. As Jiddhu Krishnamurti[1] so clearly put it, 'Observation without evaluation is the highest form of intelligence'. As Alan Watts[2] said of the Dào, 'It

---

[1] Jiddu Krishnamurti who was born on 11 May 1895 and died on 17 February 1986, was an Indian philosopher, speaker and writer who was, and still is, regarded as an enlightened man.

[2] Alan Wilson Watts, born 6 January 1915 and died 16 November 1973) was an English philosopher, writer, and speaker, who presented Eastern teachings to the West during the 1950s to early the early 1970s. His talks were taped and are still available. They are the most sublime representatives of Daoist phillosophy.

may reign, but it does not rule. It is the pattern of things but not the enforced'.[23]

This description of the inter-connectedness between all people and each with the Universe is not unique to Daoism. The great challenge of metaphysics and esoteric religions is to resolve the paradox of our being both an individual and yet all connected at the same time.

It is about finding out how to perceive and then apperceive beyond what the five senses display to the mind - and to observe how it (the mind) discriminates between subject and object and thereby discerns differences. It is more accurate to say that the quest is not to resolve the paradox of self and the world, but rather to acknowledge that this situation exists and thereby to transcend the dualistic tendencies of this discriminative mental activity.

Underpinning our attempt to understand all of this, and hence comprehend the Daoist schools of thought, is to seek to appreciate some fundamental principles. The first is that of the state of Manifestation arising from the Unmanifest. The Unmanifest is the Dào in the state of rest. For this state of rest, the creation of 阴 yīn[3] and 阳 yáng manifests as all that is observable in the Universe. This expression of yīn and yáng is further explored in an even older text known as the 易經 Yì Jīng[4] or Book of Changes.

For example, if no males existed, the naming of, and how we classify a female could not be attempted. The terms are relative to one another. The Manifest world moves through cycles: spring through to winter, night and day, and from birth to death. Everything is in motion; nothing is at rest even if it so appears. It is just how the one totally connected and interacting Dào expresses itself.

These manifestations, these objects, are all created through this interaction and are relative parts of the whole. They appear as opposites but are, in fact, just different by degree. One cannot exist

---

[3] Everyone is familiar with this now wide concept of yin and yang.
[4] There are many books with commentaries written about this. One of the best works is I *Ching Numerology* (Wade-Giles transliteration of Yì Jīng) written by Da Liu.

without the other because their expression and our classification of either can only be accomplished relatively, one through the other.

There are some metaphors that we can use to illustrate this. One good example, borrowed from Hindu metaphysics, is that of the clay being one sole substance, but having the appearance of many different types and shapes of pots. Another is that of the waves, each seemingly separate but all connected within the one ocean.

The Dào is the Substantial Reality that is both behind and moving through the phenomenal world. This is described in Daoist terminology through the energy that pervades all, the expression of the Dào. Hence, Daoists describe these things through a paradigm of energy. Although as individual human beings we are separate (or seem to be so), at the level of the phenomenal world, we are connected energetically as expressions of the Dào - the Manifest expressing itself in the phenomenal world.

As above, so below is a principle that may also be expressed as the relationship of the microcosm to the macrocosm. That is, of the person being a smaller scale version of the Universe. The aim of Daoists is therefore to try to increase their energetic vibrations so as to merge with the Unmanifest that is the Dào. This understanding and hence attention should therefore be internally directed. This cannot be achieved by the intellect. In fact, the Dào cannot really be explained by the intellect at all. It can only be experienced.

Even the Buddha[5] did not speculate about such things that cannot be known. Why does the Dào choose to express itself? If we knew, we would not have written this book, nor would you be reading it!

Daoism, however, unlike some Eastern religions and philosophies, does not abjure the body but works with it to achieve harmony with the Dào. Mind and body are inter-connected, and each affects the other. Moreover, the distinction is superficial. They are

---

[5] The Buddha was also known as Siddhattha Gotama or Siddhārtha Gautama. Upon his enlightenment and being asked what he was, he stated that he was 'awakwened.

just the different rates of energy vibration and classifications. Ultimately all is one. If you wish to worship anything, why would you not start with your own body? Your mind and body and the world are not separate things. This does not mean that you should think that only the body is 'you'. Quite the contrary, it is an ephemeral manifestation, wrongly believed to be static from the viewpoint of a moment in time.

Those extreme conceptual schools that abjure the body and tell you that the mind is all and the body is unimportant may then very well proceed to tell you that the body must be in the right position in order to meditate! This is merely a dualistic approach whilst attempting to be non-dualistic. Please beware of the risk of getting lost in these doctrinaire obfuscations. Daoism adopts a practical and holistic approach.

As a philosophy or way of life, Daoism places much importance on being natural, or living in accordance with nature or by the natural way. The Universe is understood to be integrated as a whole and human beings are a representation thereof, existing as a microcosm in relation to the macrocosm. Hence, we are not born into the world as is often stated, but quite the reverse. The world is born in us.

Lǎo Zǐ

Alongside the Bible and the Quran, The Dào dé Jīng is one of the most translated texts in history.

The first verse is arguably the most profound of all of the eighty-one verses. To understand it is to comprehend all. This is to appreciate that the Dào can be neither expressed nor understood through the prism of the Finite Mind (thinking as oneself as totally separate) nor through the Manifest, known in ancient Daoist writings as *The Ten Thousand Things*[6].

Words are produced purely as an expression of concepts, primarily using verbs and nouns to represent something that at its basic level is energy or movement. Just as a camera (or probably more likely a mobile phone!) may only represent in a static way, a fixed image of a moving event.

If we take the use of a computer, for example. I am using a laptop (hardware), a Word Processor (software), whilst thinking and typing in an attempt to describe in words the most sublime metaphysics. How many steps removed from reality is this?

Reality is several steps removed from how we even perceive it to be, let alone by how we attempt to describe it. We may write 'the apple is juicy and tasty', but what does this mean? It cannot possibly represent the actual eating of it or how the taste is experienced.

First of all, we would need to agree what the terms 'juicy' and 'tasty' actually mean. Of course, they mean different things to different people. All are relative terms, meaningless outside of context, and variable according to circumstance. Moreover, some people may not like apples at all, especially not those that are prone to spray juice all over one's freshly ironed shirts!

So, the most mystical of all experiences - to be as one with the Dào, cannot be expressed via the literal or literary medium. In actual

---

[6] The Ten Thousand Things is the term that the ancient Chinese used to describe the Manifest, the objective world. IOt means everything or more precisely, every thging.

fact, to state that you are one with the Dào, implies that there are two things. This is incorrect as there is no duality at all.

This principle is stated at the outset, in Chapter One

The Dao that can be expressed thus is not the Eternal Dao

The name that can be expressed as such is not the eternal name

This is an explanation of the limitations of language. That is, words are merely a concession to the finite or manifest mind, absorbed as it is in concept and abstract - this and that. To square the circle, the mind itself is not a thing, a noun. It is merely energy constantly expressing itself and so a noun is used to try and describe and reference it. Of course, it is in fact, impossible to write anything without using nouns. This is simply a further concession to practical expression through adherence to the conventions of a language.

When Bodhidharma, the first Chan Buddhist Patriarch[7] was sat facing the wall[8] his future successor, (later to be appointed Second Patriarch 大祖慧可 Dà Zǔ Huì Kě stood in the snow and presented his severed arm to him. This somewhat of an extreme reaction you may think (even if true) and was in response to Bodhidharma having previously refused to teach him.

He cried "Master, my mind is not pacified. 'Please, pacify my mind' Bodhidharma replied. 'If you bring me that mind, I will pacify it for you' Dà Zǔ Huì Kě replied: 'When I search for my mind I cannot find it.' Bodhidharma concluded thus: "Then your mind is thus pacified" The question is therefore; what is the mind and who is doing the searching?

---

[7] Bodhidharma came from India and founded Chan Buddhism and hence became the First Patriarch. He was said to have meditated for 9 years facing the wall.
[8]

Bodhidharma

Nothingness, the equivalent to the Buddhist notion of Emptiness does not mean a sort of nihilistic void. It means simply 'No Thing'. Essentially there are no single 'things'. Everything and everyone are inter-connected. No greater evidence of this can be found than at the present moment with the Coronavirus crisis. Yet, it is not just the palpable connectivity of human beings that is being described. It is also the oneness of consciousness, or The Absolute or God or the Dào that is being expressed.

Only by using the finite, discriminative mind do we see objects from the standpoint of subject and object. This is known as dualism and is a view from the perspective of each individual who sees the world as external and separate from his or herself.

Alan Watts puts it like this:

If you awaken from this illusion, and you understand that black implies white, self implies other, life implies death — or shall I say, death implies life — you can conceive yourself. Not conceive, but feel yourself, not as a stranger in the world, not as someone here on sufferance, on probation, not as something that has arrived here by fluke, but you can begin to feel your own existence as absolutely fundamental.

What you are basically, deep, deep down, far, far in, is simply the fabric and structure of existence itself. So, say in Hindu mythology, they say that the world is the drama of God. God is not something in Hindu mythology with a white beard that sits on a throne, that has royal prerogatives.

God in Indian mythology is the self, Satcitananda. Which means sat, that which is, chit, that which is consciousness; that which is ananda is bliss. In other words, what exists, reality itself is gorgeous, it is the fullness of total joy.

- The Nature of Consciousness;
also published as What Is Reality? (1989)

Most people see their existence as ending at the boundaries of the skin and bones of the body. Daoists, Buddhists and Advaita Vendatists, as well as others have all apperceived this not be so. That there is only one, whether expressed as Dào, Brahman, The Absolute, God or any other use of words that are wholly inadequate to fully describe this ineffable subject.

As stated, it is not just those born in the East who have understood this. To quote one of our favourite English mystical poets William Blake[9].

If the doors of perception were cleansed
Every thing would appear to man as it is, Infinite

---

[9] William Blake was born in England on 28th November 1757 and died on 2 August 1827. He was a poet, painter, and printmaker and a major force in the history of the **poetry** and visual arts of the **Romantic Movement**. His poetry reflects his metaphysical wisdom and his obvious spiritual experiences.

For man has closed himself up
Till he sees all things thro' narrow chinks of his cavern
The Marriage of Heaven and Hell[10]

So, Everything or All Things emanate from Nothingness. They are both the same. The Manifest arises from the Unmanifest. 'Form is Emptiness, Emptiness is Form' is how the Buddhist would describe this – as quoted from the Heart Sutra[11]. In other words, there are not two things at all. There is just one, but manifestation may appear to display as two. This is known as Maya in some Hindu metaphysical systems.

One sees the world through the discriminating mind, describing reality through the limited use of words reifying the subject-object dualistic view and so it seems as though the world is made up of discrete separate objects.

In Daoist thinking, because the human being is a microcosm of the Universe, when Lǎo Zǐ sometimes seems to talk about a person's body or society or the Universe, this covers all aspects. This is similar to the Hindu and Buddhist description of Indra's Net. This net exists in Indra's palace in Heaven and it extends infinitely in all directions. At each node of the net where the threads cross there is a perfectly clear gem. Each gem reflects all the others in the net.

Just as the threads of Indra's Net bind the gems together so do our physical bodies bind our minds and as do other physical entities bind other systems to the universe.

Going through the door means to surrender the mind to the consciousness, and to the awareness that observes all. Awareness exists whether one is asleep, awake or dreaming. It was there when you were born and will be there when you die.

---

[10] The Marriage of Heaven and Hell a series of texts imitating a biblical prophecy based on the writer's own personal beliefs.
i[11] The Heart Sūtra - 心經 Xīnjīng is a high level teaching in the Buddhist sutras. Its full name is "The Heart of the Perfection of Wisdom".

In fact, one sees the body age, but it still feels like they are the same person that moved from school to retirement and thus are confused by this. How can 'I' who observes illness, health, emotions, and all else possibly be the body? Or even the mind that fluctuates from moment to moment? What is observed changes without any interference and yet what remains as the observer seems never to change.

In the universe, there are things that are known, and things that are unknown, and in between, there are doors
William Blake – Songs of Innocence and Experience

And thus, again from Blake, – *Auguries of Innocence*
To see a world in a grain of sand
And a heaven in a wild flower
Hold infinity in the palm of your hand
And eternity in an hour

In the world as we perceive it, through the discriminating mind, everything is placed into binary categories. This is how the Manifest appears as is described as Yin and Yang, positive and negative. In actual fact, they are not separate, but are mutually arising and complementary.

All are relative terms. Difficult can only be relative to easy. A female can only be described as such against the concept of male, and vice-versa. It is another way of describing the wholeness of everything and its inter-relationships.

As the legendary Daoist sage 莊子 Zhuang Zi[12] puts it:

He who perceives the oneness of everything, does not know about the duality in it.

---

[12] Zhuangzi, 莊子 lived during the late 4th century BC. He is regarded as is the pivotal figure in Classical Philosophical Daoism. He wrote an equally famous and much lauded compilation of his and others' writings that was named after him – the Zhuangzi.

How do you organise your blood supply to your body or ensure that your breath continues even when you sleep? Did this 'you' that you understand yourself to be plan and organise this? Or did it happen by itself?

Again, let us reference Zhuang Zi:
From the sage's emptiness, stillness arises; From stillness, action. From action, attainment.

Zhuang Zi

The concept of 无为; wú wéi [13] or non-action is a Daoist principle that underpins its highest reasoning. The Dào that runs through and is 'you' expresses its wholeness and unity without interference or contrivance.

The function of non-action or non-interference of wú wéi is a prevailing and ubiquitous precept referenced throughout all strands of Daoism. It is a principle rarely understood. It means to refrain from striving because this causes stress and tension. Each individual seeks

---

[13] 無爲; wú wéi is pervasive amongst Chinese philosophy. The best translation we can make is perhaps, "effortless action".

to be happy. Happiness is however sought in outside objects – in one or more of the Ten Thousand Things.

William Shakespeare, another very famous English poet writes in his poem – *The Phoenix and the Turtle*[14]
Truth may seem but cannot be;
Beauty brag but 'tis not she;
Truth and beauty buried be

There is no independent existence, other than the Dào, manifesting as all 'things'. The seemingly independent objective world appears to be the ultimate, experience but it is just the outward manifestation of the Dào, a form of movement of energy within itself that appears as objects to the unawakened mind.

Each of the Ten Thousand Things – or objects is just a hollow reflection of the true happiness that solely resides in the Dào. Desire has its basis in simply wanting to eliminate itself. Once satiated, you are back where you started. People simply confuse the happiness that is inherent with the Dào with the manifestations, the Ten Thousand Things, that are fleeting and ephemeral.

True happiness cannot be found from without but only from within. It is achieved independently of objects. Once this is realised, together with the notion that external objects and internal mind are not separate, then one can stand a chance of sustaining happiness and harmony with all.

It is always the false that makes you suffer, the false desires and fears, the false values and ideas, the false relationships between people. Abandon the false and you are free of pain, truth makes you happy, truth liberates.

Nisragatta Maharaj[15]

---

[14] The Phoenix and the Turtle is an allegorical poem about the death of ideal love
[15] Nisargadatta Maharaj was born on the 17th April 1897 in India and died on 8th September 1981. Regarded as a truly enlightened teacher of Hindu non dualism.

The Dào is emptiness and formlessness, Samsara and Nirvana. It is due to its emptiness that it can contain all things. This language however is a concession to the limitations of words. It does not actually contain separate objects. There are objects as they are perceived from a dualist Subject-Object perception as the Manifest, and as the container being the Unmanifest. It is above and beyond creation, beyond time and space.

Time and Space only reside in the world of the Manifest. In actually, the Dào is beyond these limits. It cannot be known as an object because it is not such, otherwise it would not be the Dào. As this is stated in the Heart Sutra – *Form is Emptiness and Emptiness is Form*, The Manifest is not different from the UnManifest. It can be described as energy, but all descriptions inevitably fall short.

This is an explanation of the expression of the energy of the Dào as it manifests. It is without the guile and contrived cleverness of the limited mind. It is due to the effortless nature of the Dào that it is immanent, eternal, and omniscient. Having no dimensions, it can only be observed in its objective dimension, not as the Subject that it is.

The world is like a sheet of paper on which something is typed. The reading and the meaning will vary with the reader, but the paper is the common factor, always present, rarely perceived. When the ribbon is removed, typing leaves no trace on the paper. So is my mind – the impressions keep on coming, but no trace is left.

Wisdom is knowing that I am nothing
Love is knowing that I am everything
And between these two
My life moves

Nisragatta Maharaj

Time, like space is one dimension of the Dào, in its Manifest state. As Unmanifest, it is timeless. It does not have a concrete purpose for itself or a desire to manifest as these are qualities of the objects that are manifested. Having no desire results in being present whilst all manifestations arise and subside. In believing that a body and mind combination, controlled by an ego is the real self leads to missing the state of being unborn and eternal.

If you wish to transcend birth and death, going and coming, and to be freely unattached, you should recognise the Man who is at this moment listening to this talk on the Dharma. He is the one who has neither shape nor form, neither root nor trunk, and who, having no abiding place, is full of activities.

临济义玄 Línjì Yìxuán[16] known as Rinzai in Japan

Water is an oft used metaphor in spirituality, especially for Daoists. It is also beyond merely being a metaphor. Water is powerful, ubiquitous, flowing, soft and transformative. It acts without thought of results and with utmost patience. We may think that we are individuals, separate, but is a wave not just a part of the whole ocean? Water may take the form of an ice cube or an ocean or steam, but its underlying essence remains the same.

There is a way between voice and presence
where information flows.
In disciplined silence it opens.
With wandering talk it closes.

Rumi[17]

Going to excess will inevitably result in misfortune. It is much better to adopt the approach of the middle way. To live in harmony with all things requires moderation and a self-awareness. The

---

[16] Línjì Yìxuán was a famous Chan (Zen) Buddhist monk who died in 866. His birth date is unknown
[17] Born as Jalāl ad-Dīn Muhammad in September 1207. He died on the 17th December 1273. He was a 13th-century Persian poet, mystic of the Sufi order.

wealthiest people may not be the happiest or the healthiest and fear losing this wealth.

It is hard to find
A man who has an open mind,
Who neither seeks nor shuns
Wealth or pleasure,
Duty or liberation,
Life or death
He does not want the world to end,
He does not mind if it lasts.
Whatever befalls him,
He lives in happiness[18].
Also,
For he is truly blessed
Birdsong brings relief
to my longing
I'm just as ecstatic as they are,
but with nothing to say!
Please universal soul, practice
some song or something through me!

Rumi

A powerful haiku[19] by Basho[20] puts in a very few words the meaning.

When I look carefully
I see the nazuma blooming
By the hedge!

---

[18] The Heart of Awareness – A Translation of the Ashtavakra Gita – Thomas Byrom – Chapter 17, verses 6 and 7.
[19] A haiku is a very short form of Japanese poetry, now enjoying some level of popularity in the West
[20] A famous Japanese poet of the Edo period.

Finally, In the book Zen Buddhism & Psychoanalysis [21], D.T.Suzuki comes to similar conclusions about the person who follows Dao[22] written from a Zen perspective

He moves as if not moving. He illustrates the Lao-tsean doctrine of the action of non-action.

In a similar way the Zen-man is never obtrusive, but always self-effacing and altogether unassuming. While he declares himself to be "the most honoured one," there is nothing in his outward mien exhibiting his inner life. He is the unmoved mover. This is, indeed, where the real "I" emerges, not the "I" sub specie eternitatis, in the midst of the infinity. This "I" is the securest ground which we can all find in ourselves and on which we all can stand without fear, without the sense of anxiety, without the harassing moment of indecision. This "I" is negligible almost to nonexistence because it is not at all presuming and never boisterously proclaims itself to be recognised and made most of.

And so, let us allow the Eighty-One Chapters to speak to us.

---

[21] Zen Buddhism & Psychoanalysis by Erich Fromm, D.T. Suzuki & Richard Martino – published in 1960.
[22] Page 66 Fletcher & Son Limited - published version

Chapter One

道可道，非常道；名可名，非常名。

无，名天地之始；有，名万物之母。

故常无，欲以观其妙；常有，欲以观其徼。

此两者，同出而异名，同谓之玄。

玄之又玄，众妙之门。

The Dao that can be expressed as thus is not the Eternal Dao
The name that can be expressed as such is not the eternal name
Nothingness is the origin of the Heaven and Earth
Whilst existence is the root of all things
Therefore, we can go back through nothingness to observe its subtlety
We transcend Existence to observe its general shape
The two things; nothingness and existence are from the same origin
But have different names that are profound and mysterious
Even more, they are the real door through which to reveal
The secret of everything in the universe and the world.

Chapter Two

天下皆知美之为美，斯恶已；

皆知善之为之善，斯不善已。

有无相生，难易相成，长短相形，高下相盈，音声相和，前后相随。

是以圣人处无为之事，行不言之教;万物作而不为始,生而不有，为而不恃，功成而弗居。

夫唯弗居，是以不去。

Everyone in the world learns beauty as is, thus ugliness exists
Everyone in the world learns goodness as is, thus evil exists
Existence and Nothingness co-exist
Without "difficult", there is no "easy"
Without "long", there is no "short"
Without "high", there is no "low"
Without "sound", there is no "voice"
Without "before", there is no "after"

Therefore, the Sage undertakes everything without interference
Teaching others without words
So, he allows all things to grow by themselves without interference
Cultivating all things without possession
Everything is done without it being his deed
And so, he succeeds without owning the success
Because he does not claim credit, so will his success be remembered

Chapter Three

不尚贤，使民不争；

不贵难得之货，使民不为盗；

不见可欲，使民心不乱。

是以圣人之治，虚其心，实其腹，弱其志，强其骨。

常使民无知无欲。

使夫智者不敢为也。

为无为，则无不治。

Do not exalt the wise
In order to prevent people from contending
Do not treasure rare goods
In order to stop people stealing or robbing
Do not let people see objects of desire
In order to prevent people from being disturbed and tempted
Therefore, the Sage governs people by purifying their soul
Filling their bellies

Weakening their ambitions
Strengthening their bodies
He always keeps his people innocent of knowledge and desires
So that the cunning ones dare not interfere
Where there is non-interference, there is order

Chapter Four

道冲而用之或不盈。

渊兮,似万物之宗;

挫其锐,

解其纷,

和其光,

同其尘,

湛兮,

似或存。

吾不知谁之子,

象帝之先。

The Dao is formless, but its use is inexhaustible
It is fathomless like the origin of all things
Its sharpness is blunted

Its knots are untied
Its glare is tempered
All look like dust
The Dao is hidden and formless but yet it seems to exist
I don't know where it comes from
It seems to have existed before creation

Chapter Five

天地不仁，以万物为刍狗；

圣人不仁，以百姓为刍狗。

天地之间，其犹橐籥乎！

虚而不屈，动而愈出。

多言数穷，不如守中。

Heaven and Earth are not partial, they let all things run their own course
The Sage is not partial, he lets his people run their own course
Isn't the space between Heaven and Earth just like a bellows?
It is empty but cannot be exhausted
The more it works, the more it brings forth
By many words, its wit is exhausted
It is better to remain centred and silent

Chapter Six

谷神不死,

是谓玄牝。

玄牝之门,

是谓天地根。

绵绵若存,用之不勤。

The vacuity of the valley
Is a metaphor for the Dao that never dies
It is the mystical mother
The door of the mystical mother
Is the root of the Heaven and Earth
It lasts forever, and its use is inexhaustible

Chapter Seven

天长地久。

天地所以能长且久者，

以其不自生，

故能长生。

是以圣人后其身而身先；

外其身而身存。

非以其无私邪?

故能成其私。

Heaven and Earth are everlasting
The reason why they are everlasting is that they don't live for themselves
Thus, they can remain eternal
Therefore, the Sage puts himself last
And then finds himself in the foremost place for winning people's respect

Remaining aloof from gain and therefore being preserved
Is it not because of this selflessness that his Self is realised?

Chapter Eight

上善若水。

水善利万物而不争,

处众人之所恶,

故几于道。

居善地,

心善渊,

与善仁,

言善信,

政善治,

事善能,

动善时。

夫唯不争,

故无尤。

The true person's behaviour is just like water
Water benefits all things yet doesn't contend with them
Water stays in the lowest place that all have contempt for
Where it comes nearest to the Dao
The true person is good at choosing the right place
Staying calm
Getting along with others through kindness
Keeping his promises and using words with sincerity
Managing government affairs with efficiency
Business with ability
Whilst taking action at the right time
It is because he does not contend that he is blameless

Chapter Nine

持而盈之,不如其已;

揣而锐之,不可长保。

金玉满堂,莫之能守;

富贵而骄,自遗其咎。

功遂身退,天之道也。

Letting a cup overflow rather than stopping it in time
Sharpening a sword to its sharpest so that it will not last
Gold and jade filling the hall so they cannot be secured
Arrogance with wealth and honour will ruin oneself
Retire after achieving merit, this is the natural law

Chapter Ten

载营魄抱一，能无离乎？

专气致柔，能如婴儿乎？

涤除玄览，能无疵乎？

爱民治国，能无为乎？

天门开阖，能为雌乎？

明白四达，能无知乎？

（生之畜之。生而不有，为而不恃，长而不宰，是谓"玄德"。）

The soul and body are combined as one, can they unite and never be separated?
Controlling your vital essence so as to be gentle and smooth, can you return back to a state just like an infant?
Purifying your distracting thoughts and concentrating on your inner heart, can you be perfect without any defects?

Loving people and governing the country, can this be done with non-interference?

Interacting with the outside world, can you remain calm and resist temptation?

Knowing everything and possessing wisdom, can you still be knowledgeable and sensible without resorting to tricks?

Grow and nurture all things

Cultivate without possession, benefit without interference, Lead without rule

That is the mysterious virtue.

Chapter Eleven

三十辐，共一毂，当其无，有车之用。

埏埴以为器，当其无，有器之用。

凿户牖以为室，当其无，有室之用。

故有之以为利，无之以为用。

Thirty spokes are united into a hub to make a wheel
Because the hollows in the hub are joined together, this allows the wheel to turn
Moulding clay to make a vessel
Because the vessel is empty thereby usable space is created

Chapter Twelve

五色令人目盲；

五音令人耳聋；

五味令人口爽；

驰骋畋猎，

令人心发狂；

难得之货，

令人行妨。

是以圣人为腹不为目，

故去彼取此。

The five colours blind the eyes
The five musical notes deafen the ears
The five flavours spoil the taste
Horse-racing and hunting madden the mind
Rare goods make one misbehave

The Sage just feeds his belly
Rather than satisfy his senses of pleasure.
Therefore, he discards the latter and observes the former.

Chapter Thirteen

宠辱若惊,

贵大患若身。

何谓宠辱若惊?

宠为下,

得之若惊,

失之若惊,

是谓宠辱若惊。

何谓贵大患若身?

吾所以有大患者,

为吾有身,

及吾无身,

吾有何患?

故贵以身为天下,

若可寄天下；

爱以身为天下，

若可托天下。

Both favour and disfavour cause dismay
Paying too much attention to yourself causes affliction
Why be panic-stricken?
Those who receive a favour from above, are thereby placed lower
They are nervous when they receive this as they fear its loss
And then are in dismay when they lose it
This is both favour and disfavour causing panic.
What does "valuing our life like respecting what we fear" mean?
We experience fear because we have a body
Without our body, what have we to fear?
Therefore, those who can value the world as his body
Can be entrusted to the world.
For those who can love the world as his body
The world can be entrusted to his care.

Chapter Fourteen

视之不见，名曰"夷"；

听之不闻，名曰"希"；

搏之不得，名曰"微"。

此三者不可致诘，故混而为一。

其上不皦，其下不昧，绳绳兮不可名，复归于无物。

是谓无状之状，无物之象，是谓惚恍。

迎之不见其首，随之不见其后。

执古之道，以御今之有。

能知古始，是谓道纪。

Look at it but it cannot be seen - this is called "invisible"
Listen to it but it cannot be heard - this is called "inaudible"
Grasp at it but it cannot be touched - this is called "intangible"
All of these three are unfathomable, so they blend and become one
Above it is not bright

Below it is not dark

It is endless and nameless and finally returns back to nothingness

This is why it is called the form of formless, an image of nothingness, because it is elusive

Facing it you will never see its front

Following it you will never see its back

Ruling the present with the long-existent Dao

It is only through the knowledge of the Dao that one can know the origin of the universe

Chapter Fifteen

古之善为士者，微妙玄通，深不可识。夫唯不可识，故强为之容：

豫兮若冬涉川；

犹兮若畏四邻；

俨兮其若客；

涣兮其若释；

敦兮其若朴；

旷兮其若谷；

混兮其若浊；

孰能浊以静之徐清；孰能安以动之徐生。

保此道者，不欲盈。夫唯不盈，故能蔽而新成。

The ancients who were versed in the Dao were subtle and profound and too deep to be understood

They were unfathomable, so any description of them is done so only hesitantly

They were cautious as if they were crossing a river in winter

They were vigilant as if they were wary of potential attack all around

They were reserved as if they were honoured guests

They were warm as if they were melting ice

They were unsophisticated like pieces of uncarved wood

They were broad-minded like a vacant valley, obscure like muddy water

Who could be calm in turbulence and then slowly penetrate the mystery?

Who could be alert in steadiness and then slowly move forward?

Those who follow the Dao, could not rise to excess

Because they were not excessive, they could renew what was worn out

Chapter Sixteen

致虚极,守静笃。

万物并作,吾以观复。

夫物芸芸,各复归其根。归根曰静,静曰复命。复命曰常,知常曰明。不知常,妄作凶。

知常容,容乃公,公乃全,全乃天,天乃道,道乃久,没身不殆。

To reach the utmost clarity, empty your mind and avoid distracting thoughts
Keep firm to the tranquillity of your heart
All things grow naturally, and I observe the law with its endless cycles
All things grow luxuriantly, and finally return back to their root
To return back to their root is to return to a state of calm and peace that is their destiny
To return to their destiny is the eternal law
To know the eternal law is wisdom

Not to know the eternal law will create disaster
He who knows the eternal law is tolerant
Being tolerant, he can be impartial
Being impartial, he can be well-balanced
Being well-balanced, he is consistent with the nature that is the Dao
Being consistent with the Dao he will be eternal
So, can he be ever protected from harm

Chapter Seventeen

太上，下知有之；其次，亲而誉之；其次，畏之；其次，侮之。信不足焉，有不信焉。

悠兮其贵言。功成事遂，百姓皆谓："我自然。"

With the best form of governance, the people only know about the existence of their ruler
For the second best, the people get close to, and lavish praise on him
For the next best ruler, the people fear him
After that, the people insult him
If the ruler lacks credit, then he will lose people's faith
The best ruler is moderate, quiet and relaxed
And when the state affairs have been accomplished with success
His people will say: "All has been accomplished by nature"

Chapter Eighteen

大道废，有仁义；

六亲不和，有孝慈；

国家昏乱，有忠臣。

When the great Dao is discarded, the doctrine of Kind Heartedness and Justice arises
When the six relationships[23] are not harmonious, kind parents and filial sons are praised
When the state is in chaos, there are 'loyal' officials

---

[23] The six relationship are father, son, elder brother, younger brother, husband and wife.

Chapter Nineteen

绝智弃辩，民利百倍；

绝伪弃诈，民复孝慈；

绝巧弃利，盗贼无有。

此三者以为文，不足。

故令有所属：见素抱朴，少私寡欲。

Discard wisdom and rhetoric, and the people shall profit a hundredfold
Discard hypocrisy and fraudulence, and the people shall return to filial piety and kind-heartedness
Discard cunning and searching for profit, and the robbers and thieves shall disappear
All of these three are external and inadequate and they are not enough to be used to govern a state
Therefore, make the people be dependable and restrained, being unsophisticated and simple, refraining from selfishness and curtailing desires

Chapter Twenty

绝学无忧。唯之与阿,相去几何?美之与恶,相去若何?人之所畏,不可不畏。

荒兮,其未央哉!

众人熙熙,如享太牢,如春登台。

我独泊兮,其未兆,如婴儿之未孩;

傫傫兮,若无所归。

众人皆有馀,而我独若遗。我愚人之心也哉!沌沌兮!

俗人昭昭,我独昏昏。

俗人察察,我独闷闷。

澹兮其若海,飂兮若无止。

众人皆有以,而我独顽且鄙。

我独异于人,而贵食母。

Abandoning vulgar knowledge will bring freedom from trouble
What is the difference between 'yes' and 'no'?
What is the difference between 'beauty' and 'ugliness'?
That what the people fear, is indeed to be feared
The universe is so vast and seems to be endless
All people are merrymaking like enjoying a feast and mounting the terraces in spring to enjoy the scenery
I am alone and mild, remain aloof and indifferent, like an infant
who cannot smile
Friendless, like one without a home
All people have more than enough but I seem to have nothing left over
My heart must be that of a fool, that someone must think to be chaotic and nebulous
The vulgar seem to be clever and complacent, I seem to be confused and clumsy
Patient like the sea, adrift like no end
All people exploit their usefulness whist I am slow-witted and gauche
I am different from others and value the spiritual mind of the Dao

Chapter Twenty-One

孔德之容，惟道是从。

道之为物，惟恍惟惚。惚兮恍兮，其中有象；恍兮惚兮，其中有物。窈兮冥兮，其中有精；其精甚真，其中有信。

自今及古，其名不去，以阅众甫。吾何以知众甫之状哉！以此。

The mask of great virtue changes and varies with the Dao
That which is called Dao is what seems to exist or not exist
To be or not to be, enigmatic, yet within it are signs
To exist or not exist, enigmatic, yet within it are objects
It is profound and dark, but being enigmatic is its essence
The essence is so true, yet whilst enigmatic there is evidence
From ancient times to today, its name has never been erased
Whereby we can observe the origin of all things
How can we know the shapes of the origin of all things?
Through the Dao

Chapter Twenty-Two

曲则全，枉则直，洼则盈，敝则新，少则得，多则惑。

是以圣人执一为天下式。不自见，故明；不自是，故彰；不自伐，故有功；不自矜，故能长。

夫唯不争，故天下莫能与之争。古之所谓"曲则全"者，岂虚言哉！诚全而归之。

Yield, so that you may be preserved
Bend, so that you can be straight
Remain as an empty vessel, so that it can be filled
Wear out and then it can be renewed
Have little and then you can gain
Have much and you will become confused
Therefore, the Sage keeps these principles as the model of the world
He does not show himself off, therefore he is luminous
He isn't self-righteous; therefore he is prominent
He does not boast about himself, therefore he is meritorious
He is not full of pride; therefore, he can endure long
He contends for nothing, so nobody in the world can contend with him

As the old saying goes: "yield, so that you may be preserved." is definitely not empty talk

And it can truly be attained

Chapter Twenty-Three

希言自然。

故飘风不终朝，骤雨不终日。孰为此者？天地。天地尚不能久，而况于人乎？故从事于道者，同于道；德者，同于德；失者，同于失。

同于道者，道亦乐得之；同于失者，失亦乐得之。

信不足焉，有不信焉。

Using few words complies with nature
Therefore, a fierce wind cannot last a whole morning
And intense rainfall cannot continue for a whole day
Who has made this so?
Heaven and Earth
Even Heaven and Earth cannot prevail for long, so how could a human being?
So, a man follows the Dao and conforms to it
A man follows Virtue and conforms to it
A man who abandons the Dao and Virtue will lose everything

The man who conforms to the Dao is welcomed by the Dao

The man who conforms to abandonment is welcomed by abandonment

If the ruler lacks credit, then he will lose people's faith

Chapter Twenty-Four

企者不立；跨者不行；自见者不明；自是者不彰；自伐者无功；自矜者不长。

其在道也，曰：馀食赘行。物或恶之，故有道者不处。

Standing on tiptoes you cannot remain balanced
Walking with big strides you cannot go any distance
He who shows himself dims his own light
He who is self-righteous isn't prominent
He who boasts about himself isn't meritorious
He who prides himself cannot endure long
From the aspect of the Dao, all of these are metaphors for leftover foods and inappropriate and disgusting behaviour
Therefore, the man of the Dao will never act like this

Chapter Twenty-Five

有物混成，先天地生。寂兮寥兮，独立不改，周行而不殆，可以为天下母。吾不知其名，强字之曰"道"，强为之名曰"大"。大曰逝，逝曰远，远曰反。故道大，天大，地大，人亦大。域中有四大，而人居其一焉。

人法地，地法天，天法道，道法自然。

There was something nebulous that existed before Heaven and Earth
It was silent and intangible, independent, revolving eternally
It could be taken as the origin of the universe
I don't know its name so hesitantly called it "Dao" and "Great"
Being great means reaching out in space
Reaching out in space means being far away
Being far away means returning to the origin
So the "Dao" is great
Heaven is great
Earth is great

People are great

There are four greats in the universe and people are one of them

People model Earth, Earth models Heaven, Heaven models the Dao, the Dao models its own nature

Chapter Twenty-Six

重为轻根,静为躁君。

是以君子终日行不离辎重。虽有荣观,燕处超然。奈何万乘之主,而以身轻天下?

轻则失根,躁则失君。

Heaviness is the root of lightness
Stillness is the lord of restlessness
Therefore, the Sage travels all day with his provision-cart
Though enjoying a glorious and gorgeous life, he stays aloof and at ease
Why should a ruler of a big state act in haste?
Lightness will lose its root whilst rashness will cause imbalance

Chapter Twenty-Seven

善行无辙迹；善言无瑕谪；善数不用筹策；善闭无关楗而不可开；善结无绳约而不可解。

是以圣人常善救人，故无弃人；常善救物，故无弃物。是谓"袭明"。

故善人者，不善人之师；不善人者，善人之资。不贵其师，不爱其资，虽智大迷，是谓要妙。

Good deeds leave no trace
Good speakers express themselves flawlessly
Good reckoners calculate without counters
He who is good at making locks makes no use of a bolt
And yet the door cannot be opened
He who is good at knotting makes no use of a rope
And yet the knot cannot be untied
Therefore, the Sage excels at personnel placement and so there is nobody who is forgotten

He excels at making use of all things and then there is nothing abandoned
This is the inner wisdom
Thus the good man can be a teacher to the bad man whilst the bad man can be a lesson for the good man
Showing no respect to his teacher and not cherishing his lesson, he actually is a fool, though seems to be clever
Such is the subtle secret

Chapter Twenty-Eight

知其雄，守其雌，为天下蹊。为天下蹊，常德不离，复归于婴儿。

知其白，守其黑，为天下式。为天下式，常德不忒，复归于无极。知其荣，守其辱，为天下谷。为天下谷，常德乃足，复归于朴。

朴散则为器，圣人用之，则为官长，故大制不割。

Knowing well his power as a man, he still retains the tenderness of a woman
And this become the source for the whole world
Being the source for the whole world, he keeps to the eternal virtue and returns back to be like an infant
Conscious of the bright, but still keeping himself in the dark
And so this becomes the model of the world
Being a model for the world, he will never stray from the way of virtue and thus will return back to infinity

Conscious of the glory, but still keeping himself humble.
And so this becomes the valley of the world
Being the valley of the world he will be filled with eternal virtue and will return back to simplicity
As simplicity is utilised, it is shaped into a vessel
The Sage makes use of it and becomes the lord over other officials
Therefore the integrity of his rule will not be compromised

Chapter Twenty-Nine

将欲取天下而为之，吾见其不得已。天下神器，不可为也，不可执也。为者败之，执者失之。

故物或行或随；或嘘或吹；或强或羸；或培或堕。

是以圣人去甚，去奢，去泰。

If anyone desires to rule the world by force, I think that he will never succeed
The world is sacred and cannot be interfered with and controlled by force
He who interferes using force will fall
He who controls using force will lose
Everyone's character is different however
Some go ahead whilst some follow behind
Some are slow whilst some are hasty
Some are strong whilst others are weak
Some are self-loving whilst others are self-destroying
So the Sage should avoid excess, extravagance and pride

Chapter Thirty

以道佐人主者，不以兵强天下。其事好还。师之所处，荆棘生焉。（大军之后，必有凶年。）

善有果而已，不敢以取强。果而勿矜，果而勿伐，果而勿骄，果而不得已，果而勿强。

物壮则老，是谓不道，不道早已。

The man who assists his lord in harmony with the Dao, will not assert himself to conquer the world by military force
Such a course is sure to meet with its proper return
Wherever the military arrives, briar and thorns take root
A year of death is sure to be followed by a great war
A skilful commander achieves his aim and then ceases. He dares not to complete his mastery
Achieving his aim without glorying it
Achieving his aim without boasting
Achieving his aim as a matter of necessity
Achieving his aim without flaunting his force

Everything reaches its pinnacle and then is bound to decline
That which is against the Dao will soon come to an end

Chapter Thirty-One

夫兵者，不祥之器，物或恶之，故有道者不处。

君子居则贵左，用兵则贵右。兵者不祥之器，非君子之器，不得已而用之，恬淡为上。胜而不美，而美之者，是乐杀人。夫乐杀人者，则不可得志于天下矣。

古事尚左，凶事尚右。偏将军居左，上将军居右。言以丧礼处之。杀人之众，以悲哀泣之，战胜以丧礼处之。

Weapons are evil tools that are hated by all people
Therefore those aligned with the Dao do not like to employ them
The gentleman considers the left the most honourable place
In a time of a war, by contrast, the right hand is considered to be the most honourable place
For weapons are evil tools and the gentleman is unwilling to use them
He uses them only on the compulsion of necessity with a calm restraint
Even in victory, there is no pride and joy. He who is joyful and is proud of slaughter, will not be successful in the world

On occasions of auspicious omens to be on the left is the most honourable place

On occasions of ill omens, it is the right side. The assistant general is on the left side whilst the general is on the right side

That is to say, it is assigned as a rite of mourning

Slaughtering multitudes should be mourned with sorrow. A victory in a war with slaughter should be treated as a funeral rite

Chapter Thirty-Two

道常无名，朴。虽小，天下莫能臣。侯王若能守之，万物将自宾。

天地相合，以降甘露，民莫之令而自均。

始制有名，名亦既有，夫亦将知止，知止可以不殆。

譬道之在天下，犹川谷之于江海。

The Dao is nameless, eternal and without guile. Thought small, nobody in the world can conquer it

If the king and barons could hold it, the whole world would yield spontaneously

Heaven and Earth unite together and thus the sweet dew falls reaching everywhere equally without any interference from man

All things grow up and then have their names. Since there are names, there is confinement. Knowing the confinement, one can be exempt from danger

The Dao to the world is a metaphor for rivers that run into the sea

Chapter Thirty-Three

知人者智,自知者明。

胜人者有力,自胜者强。

知足者富。

强行者有志。

不失其所者久。

死而不亡者寿。

He who knows others is discerning
He who knows himself is intelligent
He who overcomes others is strong
He who overcomes himself is powerful
He who is content is rich
He who is persistent has a firm will
He who does not lose his root endures
He who dies yet his spirit remains, has longevity

Chapter Thirty-Four

大道氾兮，其可左右。万物恃之以生而不辞，功成而不有。衣养万物而不为主，（常无欲，）可名于小；万物归焉而不为主，可名为大。以其终不自为大，故能成其大。

The great Dao spreads everywhere and extends in all directions
All things depend on it for growth, but it never refuses any of them
Everything is done without it taking credit for so doing
It cultivates all things without dominating. So it may be called small
All things converge into it, but it never dominates them. So it may be called great
It never proclaims itself as great and thus it becomes so

Chapter Thirty-Five

执大象,天下往。

往而不害,安平太。

乐与饵,过客止。道之出口,淡乎其无味,视之不足见,听之不足闻,用之不足既。

He keeps to the great Dao and so all of the people follow
Following him without harming each other, they will live in peace and tranquility
Music and delicacies will make the passers-by stop
The Dao is mild to the taste
Look at it yet it cannot be seen
Listen to it yet it cannot be heard
But its use is inexhaustible

Chapter Thirty-Six

将欲歙之,必固张之;将欲弱之,必固强之;将欲废之,必固举之;将欲取之,必固与之,是谓微明。

柔弱胜刚强。鱼不可脱于渊,国之利器不可以示人。

Before he is about to contract, he is sure to first stretch out
Before he is about to weaken, he is sure to first strengthen
Before he is about to be laid low, he is sure to first rise up
Before he is about to have something taken away, he is sure to give
These are subtle omens
Softness overcomes rigidity. Fish should not be taken away from the water. Instruments for the profit of a state should not be shown to the people

Chapter Thirty-Seven

道常无为而无不为。候王若能守之，万物将自化。化而欲作，吾将镇之以无名之朴。无名之朴，夫亦将不欲。不欲以静，天下将自正。

The Dao follows the course of nature yet through it everything can be accomplished

If the king and barons could hold to it, the whole world would be in accord with its destiny and could proceed naturally

If they grow and reform naturally, they will allow desire to be restrained by the nameless simplicity that is the Dao

Using the nameless simplicity of the Dao to restrain them, they will be free from greed

Without greed, the whole world will return back to peace and all things will harmonise of their own volition

Chapter Thirty-Eight

上德不德，是以有德；下德不失德，是以无德。

上德无为而无以为；（下德无为而有以为）。

上仁为之而无以为；上义为之而有以为。

上礼为之而莫之应，则攘臂而扔之。

故失道而后德，失德而后仁，失仁而后义，失义而后礼。

夫礼者，忠信之薄，而乱之首。

前识者，道之华，而愚之始。是以大丈夫处其厚不居其薄；

处其实，不居其华。故去彼取此。

The man of high virtue doesn't show it; thus he is truly virtuous
The man of low virtue holds on to the intention of not losing it, thus he doesn't truly possess it
The man of high virtue follows nature and achieves nothing volitionally
The man of low virtue acts intentionally and has an ulterior motive
The man of high benevolence achieves something unintentionally

The man of high justice achieves something intentionally

The man of high propriety wants to show it and achieve something but gets no response. So he rolls up his sleeves to force it on to others

Therefore if the Dao is lost, virtue will be lost

If virtue is lost, benevolence is also lost

If benevolence is lost, justice is also lost

If justice is lost, propriety is also lost

Propriety shows the lack of loyalty and faith. And it is the beginning of chaos

Presenting doctrines and proprieties is the contrary to the Dao and the beginning of ignorance

Hence the noble man has a foothold that is solid and not flimsy. He dwells in the fruit, not in the flower. So he rejects the latter and accepts the former

Chapter Thirty-Nine

昔之得一者：天得一以清；地得一以宁；神得一以灵；谷得一以盈；万物得一以生；侯王得一以为天下正。

其致之也，谓天无以清，将恐裂；地无以宁，将恐废；神无以灵，将恐歇；谷无以盈，将恐竭；万物无以生，将恐灭；候王无以正，将恐蹶。

故贵以贱为本，高以下为基。是以候王自称孤、寡、不穀。此非以贱为本邪？非乎？故至誉无誉。是故不欲琭琭如玉，珞珞如石。

For those who were one with the Dao in ancient times
Heaven with the Dao was clarity
Earth with the Dao was tranquility
God with the Dao was spirituality
The valley with the Dao was fullness
All things with the Dao was growth

The princes and dukes with the Dao enabled the world to become stable

That is to say: without clarity, Heaven would break

Without tranquility, Earth would quake

Without spirituality, God would vanish

Without being full, the valley would dry up

Without growing, all things would die

Without stability, the princes and dukes would be overthrown

Therefore, humility is the root of nobility whilst the low is the foundation of the high. That is the reason why the princes and dukes call themselves "orphaned", "widowed" and "unworthy". Don't they depend on being humble? Too much success needn't be praised. Rather than being like splendid jade, be as solid as a rock

Chapter Forty

反者道之动；弱者道之用。

天下万物生于有，有生于无。

The movement of the Dao is circular
The function of the Dao is gentle
All things come from existence
Existence comes from Nothingness

Chapter Forty-One

上士闻道，勤而行之；中士闻道，若存若亡；下士闻道，大笑之。不笑不足以为道。故建言有之：

明道若昧；

进道若退；

夷道若纇；

上德若谷；

大白若辱；

广德若不足；

建德若偷；

质真若渝；

大方无隅；

大器晚成；

大音希声；

大象无形；

道隐无名。

夫唯道，善贷且成。

When the scholar of the highest level hears the Dao, he earnestly puts it into practice
When the scholar of the middle level hears the Dao, he half believes it and half doubts it
When the lowest man hears the Dao, he bursts into laughter. If it is not laughed at, it wouldn't be the Dao. And it is therefore said:
The bright Dao seems to be dark
The advancing Dao seems to be regressive
The even Dao seems to be rough
High virtue seems like a humble valley
Pure spirit seems like a dusty shell
Vast virtue seems to be insufficient
Firm virtue seems to be flimsy
The precious essence seems to be varied
The ultimate square seems like it has no corners
The most precious vessel takes the longest time to complete
The greatest sound seems to be soundless
The greatest image seems to be formless
The Dao is hidden and nameless
It is the Dao that helps and completes everything

Chapter Forty-Two

道生一，一生二，二生三，三生万物。万物负阴而抱阳，冲气以为和。

人之所恶，唯孤、寡、不穀，而王公以为称。故物或损之而益，或益之而损。人之所教，我亦教之。强梁者不得其死，吾将以为教父。

The Dao created one, one created two, two created three, and three created all things

All things have their back to the night side (Yin) and face to the sunny side (Yang). through their union and pervasion, they were harmonised

"Orphaned", "lonely", "unworthy" are disliked by others but are what the princes and dukes call themselves

Thus sometimes things are benefited by being diminished and vice-versa

I also teach others from what I have been taught

The violent will not die in accord with their natural course

And so this shall be my philosophical teaching

Chapter Forty-Three

天下之至柔,驰骋天下之至坚。无有入无间,吾是以知无为之有益。

不言之教,无为之益,天下希及之。

The softest substance in the world overcomes the hardest
What has no form sinks in that which has no opening. Thus, we know what the benefit is of observing non-interference
Teaching without words and benefiting by taking no action is hard to be attained in the world

Chapter Forty-Four

名与身孰亲？身与货孰多？得与亡孰病？

甚爱必大费；多藏必厚亡。

故知足不辱，知止不殆，可以长久。

Which one is more valuable, fame or life?
Which one is more worthy, life or wealth?
Which one is more harmful, gaining fame and wealth or losing your life?
Too much attention to your fame will expend more energy
Too much possession of wealth will lose much
Thus, a contented mind avoids disgrace
Knowing enough is enough avoids danger
Then so can one long endure

Chapter Forty-Five

大成若缺，其用不弊。

大盈若冲，其用不穷。

大直若屈，大巧若拙，大辩若讷。

躁胜寒，静胜热。清静为天下正。

The complete perfection seems like imperfection, but its use is inexhaustible
The greatest abundance seems to be empty, but its use is endless
The straightest seems to be bent
The most skilful seems to be clumsy
The most eloquent seems to be tongue-tied
Movements overcome the cold
Stillness overcomes the heat
Keeping quiet and non-interference become the guide for the world

Chapter Forty-Six

天下有道，却走马以粪。天下无道，戎马生于郊。

咎莫大于欲得；祸莫大于不知足。故知足之足，常足矣。

When the Dao prevails in the world, war-horses are sent back to farmers to use for ploughing
When the world is not in accord with the Dao, war-horses breed in the borderlands for wars
No crime is bigger than greed
No sin is bigger than insatiability
So, knowing satisfaction in the heart will provide eternal contentment

Chapter Forty-Seven

不出户，知天下；不窥牖，见天道。其出弥远，其知弥少。

是以圣人不行而知，不见而明，不为而成。

Without going out of the door, he knows the world
Without looking out of the widow, he understands the natural law
The further that one goes out, the less does one know
So the Sage knows everything without going out, understands everything without seeing, accomplishes all without any purpose of doing so

Chapter Forty-Eight

为学日益，为道日损。损之又损，以至于无为。无为而无不为。取天下常以无事，及其有事，不足以取天下。

Learning day by day will increase knowledge
Seeking the Dao day by day will diminish intrigue
Eventually, non-interference will be achieved after less and less is done
Having arrived at this point of non-interference, he can conquer the world by doing nothing
Governing the state should be by letting people take their own course
If they are compelled to do something by the adoption of severe measures, the world is already beyond his conquering

Chapter Forty-Nine

圣人常无心，以百姓心为心。

善者，吾善之；不善者，吾亦善之；德善。

信者，吾信之；不信者，吾亦信之；德信。

圣人在天下，歙歙焉，为天下浑其心，百姓皆注其耳目，圣人皆孩之。

The Sage has no individual opinion or mind, he regards his people's opinions and minds as his own
I treat those good people well whilst also treat those who are bad equally so
And thus, all of them become and remain good
I trust those honest people whilst I also trust the liars
And thus, all of them become and remain trustworthy
The Sage dwelling in the world restrains his opinions and mind
And enables his people to be unsophisticated
The people focus on their wisdom whist the Sage regards them as his children

Chapter Fifty

出生入死。生之徒，十有三；死之徒，十有三；人之生，动之于死地，亦十有三。夫何故？以其生生之厚。

盖闻善摄生者，陆行不遇兕虎，入军不被甲兵；兕无所投其角，虎无所用其爪，兵无所容其刃。夫何故？以其无死地。

When given to birth, men live
When buried in the earth, men die
The living are three in ten. The dead are three in ten
There are also three in ten who desperately want to live but extending themselves tend to death. Why?
Because of their excessive endeavour for an extended life.
It is said that one who is skilful in preserving his life, will not meet rhinoceros and tigers on land nor be wounded in war
The rhinoceros has no way to use its horns
The tiger has no way to use its claws, the weapon has no way to thrust its point. Why?
Because death finds no place for him

Chapter Fifty-One

道生之，德畜之，物形之，势成之。

是以万物莫不尊道而贵德。

道之尊，德之贵，夫莫之命而常自然。

故道生之，德蓄之；长之育之；亭之毒之；养之覆之。生而不有，为而不恃，长而不宰，是谓"玄德"。

All things grow in accord with the Dao, are nourished by Virtue, then take form, and then mature by external influence and environment
Thus all things respect the Dao and value Virtue
The reason is that they act in a state of non-interference and in compliance with spontaneity and nature
Therefore, all things are created by the Dao and nourished by Virtue
Grown up and developed, completed and matured, protected and maintained
Cultivate without possessing, benefit without interference, lead without rule, that is the mysterious virtue

Chapter Fifty-Two

天下有始，以为天下母。既得其母，以知其子；既知其子，复守其母，没身不殆。

塞其兑，闭其门，终身不勤。开其兑，济其事，终身不救。

见小曰明，守柔曰强。用其光，复归其明，无遗身殃；是为袭常。

The universe has a beginning, that is considered as its root
If you know the root, you will know everything
If you know everything, and hold to the root, you will be out of danger all your life
Block the orifice of desire, close its door, and then you will be free
Unlock the orifice, be busy about affairs, and then your whole life is beyond redemption
The perception of a subtle beginning is clear-sighted
The retention of softness creates strength
Use the light, and go back to illuminate your inner mind, and you will be free from disaster
This is the eternal Dao

Chapter Fifty-Three

使我介然有知，行于大道，唯施是畏。

大道甚夷，而人好径。朝甚除，田甚芜，仓甚虚；服文彩，

带利剑，厌饮食，财货有馀；是为盗夸。非道也哉！

If I have only a little knowledge, then when I am walking on the road, I will be afraid of going astray

The road is level and easy to walk on, but some people love the byways

The imperial government is corrupt. The farmland is deserted. The granary stores are empty

They wear ornamented robes, carry fine swords, are gluttonous with foods and drinks, have a superabundance of property and wealth; They can be called thieves and robbers

How far do they stray from the Dao

Chapter Fifty-Four

善建者不拔，善抱者不脱，子孙以祭祀不辍。

修之于身，其德乃真；修之于家，其德乃余；修之于乡，其德乃长；修之于邦，其德乃丰；修之于天下，其德乃普。

故以身观身，以家观家，以乡观乡，以邦观邦，以天下观天下。吾何以知天下然哉？以此。

A well planted tree cannot easily be uprooted
A firm grasp doesn't easily slip
Following the Dao, his descendants will not fall and will forever continue to sacrifice to their ancestors
Cultivating himself, Virtue is real
Cultivating the family, Virtue is abundant
Cultivating the village, Virtue is multiplied
Cultivating the state, Virtue prospers
Cultivating the world, Virtue is widespread
Therefore, from myself, I can observe others
From my family, I can observe other families
From my village, I can observe other villages

From my state, I can observe other states
From the world, we can observe the world
How could I know the world? By this way

Chapter Fifty-Five

含德之厚，比于赤子。蜂虿虺蛇不螫，攫鸟猛兽不搏。骨弱筋柔而握固。未知牝牡之合而朘作，精之至也。终日号而不嗄，和之至也。

知和曰常，知常曰明。益生曰祥。心使气曰强。物壮则老，谓之不道，不到早已。

The man who is rich in Virtue, is just like an infant
Bees, scorpions and poisonous snakes will not harm him
Wild birds and beasts of prey will not attack him
His muscles and bones are soft and weak, but his grip is strong
Not knowing the union of male and female, his penis is naturally erect
Showing his vigour is enough
Crying all day yet his throat doesn't get hoarse
Showing an accordance with harmony
Knowing harmony is knowing the law of eternity
Knowing the law of eternity is discerning and bright
Indulging in pleasures and extended life will turn to disasters

The mind that is controlled by desire is assertive
When reaching full strength, they become old
This is acting contrary to the Dao and so will soon finish them

Chapter Fifty-Six

知者不言，言者不知。

塞其兑，闭其门，挫其锐，解其纷，和其光，同其尘，是谓"玄同"。故不可得而亲，不可得而疏；不可得而利，不可得而害；不可得而贵，不可得而贱。故为天下贵。

He who is wise doesn't speak
He who says a lot is not wise
Block the orifice of desire, close its door
Its sharpness is blunt
Its tangle cannot be untied
Its glare is tempered
All look like dust
This is the mysterious unity
So, he does not discern any difference between close and afar
Between advantages and disadvantages
Between gentleness and simplicity
So, he is honoured in the world

Chapter Fifty-Seven

以正治国，以奇用兵，以无事取天下。吾何以知其然哉？以此：

天下多忌讳，而民弥贫；民多利器，国家滋昏；人多伎巧，奇物滋起；法令滋彰，盗贼多有。

故圣人云："我无为，而民自化；我好静，而民自正；我无事，而民自富；我无欲，而民自朴。"

Ruling a state in harmony with the Dao
Using troops with unexpected strategies
Governing the world without troubling the people
How do I know this? Through this:
The more prohibitions there are, the poorer the people become
The more weapons there are, the more turbulent the state becomes
The more intrigues the people create, the more evil will occur
The more statutes there are, the more thieves there will be
So, the Sage says: I do nothing, and people will reform by themselves
I love peace and quiet and people will take their right course

I do not interfere, and people will become rich by themselves

I have no greed and desires and people will be simple and unadorned

Chapter Fifty-Eight

其政闷闷，其民淳淳；其政察察，其民缺缺。

祸兮，福之所倚；福兮，祸之所伏。孰知其极？其无正。正复为奇，善复为妖。人之谜，其日固久。

是以圣人方而不割，廉而不刿，直而不肆，光而不耀。

The government is tolerant, and the people are unsophisticated
The government is severe, and the people are cunning
Misfortune may be a blessing in disguise and vice versa
Who knows the final results?
There are no definite answers
Right can turn out to be wrong, kindness can turn out to be evil
It will be a long time before people understand the confusion
Therefore, the Sage is upright but not disrespectful of others, shaping but not hurting others, straightforward but not licentious, bright but not dazzling

Chapter Fifty-Nine

治人事天，莫若啬。

夫唯啬，是谓早服；早服谓之重积德；重积德则无不克；无不克则莫知其极；莫知其极，可以有国；有国之母，可以长久；是谓深根固柢，长生久视之道。

The best way to govern a state is sparingly
Acting sparingly is to prepare early
To do early preparation is one of continuing accumulation
A continuing accumulation will be invincible
Being invincible makes others undervalue his power
Not being valued, he can rule a state
With the Dao to rule a state can long endure
This is the way to be firmly rooted and its enduring life shall be long witnessed

Chapter Sixty

治大国，若烹小鲜。

以道莅天下，其鬼不神；非其鬼不神，其神不伤人；非其神不伤人，圣人亦不伤人。夫两不相伤，故德交归焉。

Governing a state is like cooking a small fish
Ruling the world in accordance with the Dao, he will find that evil spirits lose their power
Not only will the evil spirits lose their power, but the gods will not use their power to hurt people
Not just that the gods will not use their power to harm people, the Sage will also not cause any harm to people
Therefore, they do not hurt each other, and their good influence will manifest as Virtue.

Chapter Sixty-One

大邦者下流，天下之牝，天下之交也。牝常以静胜牡，以静为下。

故大邦以下小邦，则取小邦；小邦以下大邦，则取大邦。故或下以取，或下而取。大邦不过欲兼畜人，小邦不过欲入事人。夫两者各得所欲，大者宜为下。

A great state should lie low like a river basin, like the moderation of a female, that is the concourse of the world
The female often overcomes the male by her composure and thereby achieves the low position
Therefore, if a big state is reasonable with regard to a smaller one, it will gain the approval of the small state
If a small state is modest with a big state, it will gain the favour of the big state
So sometimes they augment each other in this case or that
The big state just wants to shelter the small state, whilst the small state just wants to adhere to the big state
So, as both of them get what they want, the big state ought especially to be reasonable

Chapter Sixty-Two

道者万物之奥。善人之宝，不善人之所保。

美言可以市，尊行可以加人。人之不善，何弃之有？故立天子，置三公，虽有拱璧以先驷马，不如坐进此道。

古之所以贵此道者何？不曰：求以得，有罪以免邪？故为天下贵。

The Dao is the refuge of the universe
It is the good man's treasure and the bad man's refuge
Good words can be used for social contact, good deeds can be esteemed by others
Even bad men will not be abandoned by the Dao
When crowning a king, appointing three ministers, rather than royal etiquette with jades and teams of horses, it would be better to send the Dao as a gift
Why did our ancestors value the Dao?
Was it not because it can grant whatever is requested and people can be exempted from their guilt?
Therefore, it is cherished by the world

Chapter Sixty-Three

为无为，事无事，味无味。

大小多少，报怨以德。图难于其易，为大与其细；天下难事，必作于易，天下大事，必作于细。是以圣人终不为大，故能成其大。

夫轻诺必寡信，多易必多难。是以圣人尤难之，故终无难以。

Accomplishing without doing anything, operating without interference, tasting no flavour
What is big comes from what is small, what is plenty comes from what is few, render good to evil
Dealing with difficulties should start from the easy
Dealing with the great should start from the small
All difficulties in the world are sure to be handled from the easy, all great things in the world are sure to be handled from the small
Therefore, the Sage who never attempts to be great, finally can become great
Make a promise lightly and you will break it easily
View things as easy and you will face more troubles

Because the Sage regards all things as difficult, he never has any problems.

Chapter Sixty-Four

其安易持，其未兆易谋。其脆易泮，其微易散。为之于未有，治之于未乱。

合抱之木，生于毫末；九层之台，起于累土；千里之行，始于足下。

为者败之，执者失之。是以圣人无为故无败；无执故无失。

民之从事，常与几成而败之。慎终如始，则无败事。

是以圣人欲不欲，不贵难得之货；学不学，复众人之所过，以辅万物之自然而不敢为。

It is easy to be retained when it is at rest
It is easy to cope before omens appear
It is easy to break when it is weak
It is easy to scatter when it is tiny
Prepare before anything happens
Handle things before disorder arrives
A huge tree that fills one's arms grows from a tiny seedling; a nine-

storied tower rises from a heap of earth; a thousand li journey starts with the first step

Acting with force, will result in failure

Grasping with ideology, will lead to loss

Therefore, the Sage takes no action, so he doesn't fail, grasps with nothing so he doesn't lose

People often fail when the task is almost complete

To avoid failure, be as cautious at the end as at the beginning,

So the Sage pursues no desires, regards rare goods as having no value, learns what others don't want to learn, and remedies people's faults

Following his true nature, he assists all things by non-interference

Chapter Sixty-Five

古之善为道者，非以明民，将以愚之。

民之难治，以其智多。故以智治国，国之贼；不以智治国，国之福。

知此两者亦稽式。常知稽式，是谓"玄德"，玄德深矣，远矣，与物反矣，然后乃至大顺。

The ancient ones who excelled at following the Dao didn't teach people to be clever but to be unsophisticated
The people are difficult to govern because they are too clever
So, it is disastrous to govern a state by cleverness; it is blessed to govern a state without cleverness
Knowing the difference between the two is knowing the way of governing a state
Keeping the rule is the mysterious Virtue, which is too profound and far-reaching
Return to the original nature with all things and this shall lead to great harmony.

Chapter Sixty-Six

江海之所以能为百谷王者，以其善下之，故能为百谷王。
是以圣人欲上民，必以言下之；欲先民，必以身后之。是以圣人处上而民不重，处前而民不害。是以天下乐推而不厌。以其不争，故天下莫能与之争。

The reason why rivers and seas can be the kings of all valleys is that they take the lower position and therefore receive all valley streams
Therefore, if the Sage wants to govern people, he should be modest and humble towards them
If the Sage wants to be the model of the people, he should put his interests below those of the people
So, the Sage may be above, but his people don't feel burdened, be forward but his people don't feel at risk
The people delight to exalt him and don't weary of him
Because he doesn't create conflict, no one can compete with him

Chapter Sixty-Seven

天下皆谓我:"道大,似不肖。"夫唯大,故似不肖。若肖,久矣其细也夫!

我有三宝,持而保之。一曰慈,二曰俭,三曰不敢为天下先。

慈故能勇;俭故能广;不敢为天下先,故能成器长。

今舍慈且勇;舍俭且广;舍后且先;死矣!

夫慈,以战则胜,以守则固。天将救之,以慈卫之。

The whole world says to me: the Dao is too great to be any tangible thing
Because it is great, it doesn't seem like any imaginable thing
If it were like anything, it would have been small for a long time
I have three treasures that I hold and cherish: the first is benevolence, the second is thriftiness, the third is that I don't take precedence over others
Using benevolence I can be bold; thriftiness and I can be generous; not taking precedence over others I can be the leader of the world
Now they abandon benevolence to be bold, abandon thriftiness to be

generous, abandon the hindmost place to be the foremost

All of this ends in death

With benevolence, one can get victory in a battle, be firmly protected in defence

Heaven will save and protect him with its benevolence.

Chapter Sixty-Eight

善为士者，不武；善战者，不怒；善胜敌者，不与；善用人者，为之下。是谓不争之德，是谓用人，是谓配天，古之极也。

Adept in commanding, he doesn't show off his power
Adept in fighting, he doesn't show any rage
Adept in defeating, he still keeps away from conflict
Adept at dealing with people, he shows only his modesty to them
Therefore, this is called the Virtue of "not striving for" and is a personal strategy that follows nature
It is the supreme rule from ancient times.

Chapter Sixty-Nine

用兵有言："吾不敢为主，而为客；不敢进寸，而退尺。"

是谓行无行；攘无臂；扔无敌；执无兵。

祸莫大于轻敌，轻敌几丧吾宝。

故抗兵相若，哀者胜矣。

A master of the art of war says
I don't dare to take the initiative in attack but to take the defensive
I don't dare to advance an inch but rather would retreat a foot
This is the marshalling that looks like it has no ranks
Fighting that looks like it is without arms
Confronting enemies but seeming like having no enemies
Holding the weapons but appearing to be without weapons
No disaster is greater than underestimating the enemy that will lead to almost losing my three treasures
Therefore, when two enemies meet
The oppressed army fighting with desperate courage is sure to win

Chapter Seventy

吾言甚易知，甚易行。天下莫能知，莫能行。

言有宗，事有君。夫唯无知，是以不我知。

知我者希，则我者贵。是以圣人被褐怀玉。

What I said is easy to understand, and easy to practice
Yet no one in the world can understand or is able to practice it
What I said is well-aimed, what I have done is well-grounded
It is because they don't know this, that they don't understand me
Since few people know me, fewer of them will follow my advice
Therefore, the Sage wears coarse cloth and carries jade in his bosom.

Chapter Seventy-One

知不知，尚矣；不知知，病也。圣人不病，以其病病。夫唯病病，是以不病。

To know and yet think we do not know is advantageous
Not to know and yet think we do know is disadvantageous
The Sage has no disadvantages because he regards disadvantages as disadvantageous
And so because he regards disadvantages as disadvantageous, he has no disadvantages

Chapter Seventy-Two

民不畏威,则大威至。

无狎其所居,无厌其所生。夫唯不压,是以不厌。

是以圣人自知不自见;自爱不自贵。故去彼取此。

When the people do not fear the power of the ruler, greater disaster will come

Do not interfere with their household affairs, do not deprive people of their livelihoods

Only when the ruler doesn't deprive his people, will they not be weary of him

Therefore, the Sage desires to know himself and doesn't show off, has self-respect but doesn't value himself

So, he rejects the latter and accepts the former.

Chapter Seventy-Three

勇于敢则杀，勇于不敢则活。此两者，或利或害。天之所恶，孰知其故？（是以圣人尤难之。）

天之道，不争而善胜，不言而善应，不召而自来，繟然而善谋。天网恢恢，疏而不失。

He who is brave and favours daring is doomed to death
He who is brave and acts in tenderness will endure
There are some advantages and disadvantages between the two Why does Heaven become weary of this?
Who can tell the reason?
Even to the Sage it feels like a difficult question
The Heaven's Dao is good at overcoming without strife
Adept at responding without words
Making an appearance without calling
Achieving results without obvious design
The net of Heaven has large mesh, but it lets nothing through

Chapter Seventy-Four

民不畏死，奈何以死惧之？若使民常畏死，而为奇者，吾将得而杀之，孰敢？

常有司杀者杀。夫代司杀者杀，是谓代大匠斫。夫代大匠斫者，希有不伤其手矣。

The people do not fear death, so why threaten them with it? Supposing that the people do have a fear of death, those who do evil would be captured and killed, then who would dare to do so?
Mortality should only be the preserve of nature
And if the ruler takes the place of nature to do any killing, it is like a layman attempting to do carpentry when not being a great carpenter
He who handles carpentry when not being a great carpenter seldom escapes from injuring his hands.

Chapter Seventy-Five

民之饥,以其上食税之多,是以饥。

民之难治,以其上之有为,事以难治。

民之轻死,以其上求生之厚,是以轻死。

夫难无以生为者,是贤于贵生。

The people suffer from famine, because the rulers levy too many taxes
Because of the excessive interference from the rulers, the people are hard to govern
The people are not afraid of death, because they are anxious to make a living
So those rulers who live pure and simple lives without interfering in people's lives are wiser than those who overvalue their lives

Chapter Seventy-Six

人之生也柔软，其死也坚强。

草木之生也柔脆，其死也枯槁。

故坚强者死之徒，柔弱者生之徒。

是以兵强则灭，木强则折。

强大处下，柔弱处上。

When a man is alive, his body is soft and tender
When a man is dead, his body is hard and stiff
When trees and plants are alive, they are soft and flexible
When they are dead, they are withered and stiff
Therefore, hardness belongs to death, softness belongs to life
So, he who relies on the power of force will be lost. When the trees mature, they will be cut down
The big and strong adopt the low position while the tender and weak are placed above

Chapter Seventy-Seven

天之道，其犹张弓与？高者抑之，下者举之；有馀者损之，不足者补之。

天之道，损有馀而补不足。人之道，则不然，损不足以奉有馀。

孰能有馀以奉天下，唯有道者。

是以圣人为而不恃，功成而不处，其不欲见贤。

Is the Dao of Heaven just like the bending of a bow?
When it is too high, it is lowered
When it is too low, it is raised up
Reduce the excessive and supplement the deficient
The Dao of Heaven reduces the excess and makes up the deficiency
The Dao of Heaven is different in that it cuts down the deficient and makes up the excessive.
Who can have enough and serve the world?
Only the man of the Dao
Therefore, the Sage does everything without it being his own deed,

succeeds without owning the success
He doesn't want to show off his ability and wisdom.

Chapter Seventy-Eight

天下莫柔弱于水，而攻坚强者莫之能胜，以其无以易之。

弱之胜强，柔之胜刚，天下莫不知，莫能行。

是以圣人云："受国之垢，是谓社稷主；受国不祥，是谓天下王。"正言若反。

There is nothing softer in the world than water, but nothing is superior when it involves conquering the hard
Nothing can take its place
The weak conquers the strong, the tender conquers the hard
Everyone knows it but no one can do it
Therefore, the Sage says: "he who can bear the humiliations of the state, can be the preserver of the state"
He who can bear the disasters of the state, can be called the king of the world
True words seem to be paradoxical

Chapter Seventy-Nine

和大怨，必有馀怨；(报怨以德)，安可以为善？

是以圣人执左契，而不责于人。有德司契，无德司彻。

天道无亲，常与善人。

Following the seeming reconciliation of a deep resentment, there must still remain a grudge
Can this be the proper way?
Therefore, the Sage keeps the receipt for the loan but doesn't ask for it to be repaid
The man with Virtue is as tolerant as the Sage who keeps the receipt of the loan
The man without Virtue is as harsh as the Tax Collectors
The Dao of Heaven is impartial and will always provide help for good men

Chapter Eighty

小国寡民。使有什伯人之器而不用；使民重死而不远徙。虽有舟舆，无所乘之；虽有甲兵，无所陈之。使民复结绳而用之。甘其食，美其服，安其居，乐其俗。邻国相望，鸡犬之声相闻，民至老死，不相往来。

In a small state with a small population, even though there are all kinds of tools, people don't employ them
Let the people value their lives and not wander far away
Even though there are boats and carriages, they don't use them
Even though there is armour and weaponry, there are no opportunities to display them
Let the people return to keeping records by tying knots
The people enjoy their food, wear beautiful clothes, are satisfied with their homes and delight in their customs
The neighbouring states overlook each other and can hear the cocks crow and dogs bark
So, the people for their whole lives stay there and do not have to go out of their country and thus avoid chaos.

Chapter Eighty-One

信言不美，美言不信。

善者不辩，辩者不善。

知者不博，博者不知。

圣人不积，既以为人己愈有，既以与人己愈多。

天之道，利而不害；人之道，为而不争。

True words are not beautiful, beautiful words are not true
Kind people don't cause disputes, the people who dispute are not kind
The man who really understands does not use encyclopaedic knowledge
The man who possesses encyclopaedic knowledge cannot deeply understand things
The Sage doesn't accumulate
The more he helps others, the more abundance he possesses
The more he gives, the more he has
The heaven's Dao is beneficial without harm
The Sage's Dao is to help without striving

www.ingramcontent.com/pod-product-compliance
Lightning Source LLC
Chambersburg PA
CBHW040834190426
43197CB00045B/2954